Born and brought up in Birmingham, John Goodby has lived since his late teens in Yorkshire, Ireland, and Wales, where he currently lectures in English literature at Swansea University. He has written extensively on Irish, Welsh and English poetry, and his own poetry has appeared in *Angel Exhaust, Stand* and *Poetry Review*, among other journals. His poetry translations include Heine's *Germany: A Winter's Tale* (Smokestack, 2005) and, with Tom Cheesman, Adel Guémar's *State of Emergency* (Arc, 2007). He is the artistic director of the Boiled String poetry performance troupe and co-organiser with Lyndon Davies of the annual Hay-on-Wye Poetry Jamboree.

Also by John Goodby

Poetry
A Birmingham Yank
uncaged sea
Wine Night White

Translations
Heinrich Heine: *A Winter's Tale*
Solëiman Adel Guémar: *State of Emergency*
                    (with Tom Cheesman)

Criticism
Irish poetry since 1950: from stillness into history
Dylan Thomas: New Casebook (with Chris Wigginton)

Illennium

John [signature]

John Goodby

For Sophie with warmest best wishes – examples of 'the lyric / As shame management'!

1.iii.2019

Shearsman Books
Exeter

First published in the United Kingdom in 2010 by
Shearsman Books Ltd
58 Velwell Road
Exeter EX4 4LD

www.shearsman.com

ISBN 978-1-84861-094-1
First Edition

Copyright © John Goodby, 2010.

The right of John Goodby to be identified as the author of this work has been asserted by him in accordance with the Copyrights, Designs and Patents Act of 1988.
All rights reserved.

Acknowledgements
Acknowledgements are made to *Stand* and *Angel Exhaust* where some of these poems originally appeared.

Illennium

For Steve Vine

But [s/he] risks what former lovers risk whenever the Beloved is present, in fact or in word: deepest possibilities for shame, for sense of loss renewed, for humiliation and mockery.
—Thomas Pynchon, *Gravity's Rainbow*

Shame knowledge may allow researchers to make visible what is usually invisible, the actual state of any relationship where dialogue is available.
—Thomas J. Scheff, 'Shame as the Master Emotion of Everyday Life'

A young girl, who was blown out to sea on a set of inflatable teeth, was rescued by a man on an inflatable lobster. A coastguard spokesman commented: 'This sort of thing is all too common these days.'
—*The Times*, 1998

I

Whitehead is gone and the New Steady Statesman is kaput
whose theory I loved as a child.
As ghosts of beard & belly, they went bang.
Could this never have not-been? He felt
as if he would dearly like to smack this unpredictable
America, as a carp accomplishes the size of its pool—
Now sure pandemonium hits the square fan.
So? Cut up's corny; but that's what I am
While plagiarism is required. Cut up I mean
Progress implies it. That succumbs
the raining spectacle (out in South-West Wales)
a naff dialectic—& even if you're right you're wrong—
yet 'Formidable, affable, durable' lovely
hubristic summery self-summary just months before he died

II

The vodka jelly arrived without you at the party. Pity.
It was blue! Though I would retaliate—
a sonnet one more than a baker's dozen
undesigning gifts on your supernal grinning candour,
(Yeah. Eye-candy, you smoking dog!) The Westbourne
Concealed in rotten smoaks
In *Frenzy*, blondes wearing antique underwear
are vividly hidden, self-referentially strangeled in it.
Zephyrs, Zodiacs & Avengers cruise London streets
in sunlight, a *tsunami* of booze & sparklers. Was I 13 then?
Her long hair glossed the crown of the settee
Nigel is harping on about Kubrick's *Eyes Wide Shut*
and she is not watching Zodiacs   hear
her make water, in darkness, in the rafters of the house.

III

He sees through me as if I was America
were our faces at the centre of it, side to smiling side!
Stan, Chris, Donna, Sarah, Ivan (about to
urghh) Dear Louisiana: from the salt-stinging estuary
it is 2:17 p.m., Laugharne, steps down from the Boathouse—
24 August 1998. Sunday grey sea-smirr, the usual
but not the Greenways. You & me (still
a screwdriver the key to the *tŷ bach* door
hand-helped, up the hill—antique underwear
Avengers cruise London streets in sunlight
to respect the trust involved in a relationship—
So days after (angry June dawns) would see me
inside & out   Drenched in the not as yet 'that'
which grew a culture of his death under glass.

IV

You may well inform me of sweet damaged Dave's grave
declaration in Mozart's. He loved you
to unfold from your grin-creased filtrum   Not quite
understanding why! But why you might beard
on behalf of younger beards gives me no pause for thought
Call me Jude the Obtuse, but I drink
I might wind up in his attic shape
proffer abashed 'The Harbor Dawn' &
have to be helped up, the hill—antique, Fruit
that's less soft, but one apiece (4)   as
transgressive-yet-dependent. Song unconfessional.
To be close is close enough this weather
Sodium orange. Old Joy-Whose-Hand-Is-Ever-At-His-Hips
glows jonquil jodhpur majolica Badajoz—Chopped

V

Ideologically-emitted smiles all round
at the launch of *Yank*   In The Stick & Carrot
fleeing Kosovans and burning tanks. Confusing
speed with bacon   pulverizes
poetic articulation   eye-candy
The spin isn't wooden, it's plywooden—
O, let not her eyes speak of the Ideal any longer
of Harry H. Corbett's 'You *dirty*
slack shape waved like the sea—
'hi clare, how can i take mad john seriously
(hardly dared notice noticing you   *Eyes Wide Shut*
for fear of a cloud of shame markers ...
motes dancing in the warm & sunny Queens
shafts for your soft lips to open them for me Mumbles

VI

ARSE
    (*after Rimbaud*)

The Real too prickly, I'd moor the old oyster-grey
Vulvo atop white Hawthorn—my character sliding
towards her attic. A great, slate-plumaged bird, fretting
on the fire-trap ceiling, wings trailing in gloom.
Or standing at the baldachin bearing its gewgaws
(not to mention the masterpiece of her body!), a bear
with violet gums & sable-o'er-silvered fur. Eyes
sparbelling from the gold-whorled Kilner jars
ranged alongalong the console. And swift
dissolve—phew!—to shadow and fierce aquarium.
So days after (angry June dawns) would see me
back in the this-side clover, a donkey now,
braying grievances—in time for those suburban
Sabines to arrive & fling their arms around my neck.

VII

It smells of cellar, your new address, & joss.
Christ. 'I'll come on Friday, anyway,
hopefully armed with doughnuts.'
Hi Anjou: It is 6.13 p.m., Abertawe Mean Term Time,
hurrying past the superhuman cries of the sea
to change a red lightbulb
for a pearl. Hola, La Jolla: 'Writing an email
is like making love to a beautiful woman'
& every day   you write
the unpickupable *From Eire to Modernity*.
I couldn't undo it. Never. Not with so much to prove,
to unfold from your grin-creased filtrum cycle-
sprints, shamelessness, showers!
The heart an organ for pulling out the stops

VIII

Remembering an entire day of coffee breaks breaks
the heart   On a bike from Schmoo's
'Love is a babe', quotes Miami
Vine 'affable' lovely
(of Chris's christening!) Bernard mouths 'Sausages',
The ambush of young days   Dusk's
grape-purple amphitheatre rears up
sweating, blanching, blinking, tremor of the hand
absentmindedness and malaprops   None
of that! Raw tales, too, of damnéd Mozart's—
Pedro a Gents blowjob   carrot-sick
violet gums &   Shyness: the dazed
sensation, dryness of the mouth, terseness of
Subjects had 'emotional reactions to their emotions'.

IX

Waging Just But Only Just War from two miles up
is like making love to a beautiful woman
'If anyone's going to get hurt it has to be we and
Progress implies it. That succumbs
so Nia & yet so far. Weak
in proportion to power, brutal in its indiscriminations,
a Massive embrace of *The Week-End*
Michelle Scragg Mumbles
for a pearl. I am no thing but affect
out of her cycling shorts   hopefully with armed
                                                                       doughnuts.'
So take but we three steps from feathers to iron—
Adult our dark warmth. A taxi's kryptonite-green dash-glow
and swinging furry dice hurry
to Oystermouth's glittery necklace of bay, & furbelow

X

By the seafront a freckled girl stands—
my living daughter Katie, my dead sister Joanne—
leans on the seawall clutching *Collected Poems*   a smile
in wine-dark corduroy
and that is so anguish there as to brush that hair
whose theory I loved as a child
or brush it for her. She as an Aspect of Poetics
a simile assimilated   anacolouthon to zeugma
Beyond September Port Talbot softened as so often
by wind.   Lie thou, Ted, now.
I am certain of nothing but the hollyness of the herd's inflictions.
To be close is close enough this weather
The wicked little mystery!
Just fyi   'i looked in the mirror just now and didn't
                                                     recognise myself.'

XI

Not Humpty   but a makeless wife
She bended then 'Her kissing breasts / Touch-raptured!'
A lost   paradise   of lips   Eyes
earned the reward of one of his delighted stares
So? Embarrassment delightfully underwrites
shamefastness   The Real too prickly
'I'll kissing snatch / Thee into endless heaven' after the
                                                             school run
and didn't recognise myself. Where else can we go
Not with so much to prove
to make water? Grave's dave
declaration is done, we have to tell no-one
everwhere. Son of Sleepless Illusion
Hand mine seeking across   carpet   bombing
the integrity of the student's study and assessment

XII

Jackie told me how she was with you when
blindfoldingly sweet in 224   furiously
I can't help wanting. You with me now
support Sexual Liberation
for 4 days of fugues, foreskins and mad beryls
romantic fiendships   ululate uncontrollably
brilliantly pointless though it is
So?   Bright Starr
'(still heavily plastered)' breaks out
transferred from the White House to the Pentagon
a bad, cold-blooded   bit of clarity today
Midnight. Songs altercate in the soft
With white & bristly beard
To a peach nobody   *from your ending wish it*

XIII

Your *Hoofers'* labours—loaves like *feuillemort*
crisp Under the Spelling Wall
Dumb presagers 'so that's ok then!'
We'll split a Belash veg biryani   loosely
blush in 224   furiously refurbish
old men of less truth than tongue
Maniacs for happiness, me with my soul
she with   My dream Years unregretted from rough mugs
Brilliant, slender, slant one, everyone knows who
'traumatic irruption of eventhood' High
Street Station   brighton simon
'(still heavily plastered)'   Nigel
making a point about Benjamin in Mike Nicholls'
The Graduate   Though I would retaliate

XIV

There's buggery in the love that can be reckoned
you reck recklessly   like
songs that altercate in the soft   rebuff
Extra Strong Mints proffered during Finals
Harry H. Corbett relishing 'You *dirty*
Flagrant sweet slim legs   atop white Hawthorn
In the downpour   ache & throe
out of her cycling shorts somewhat
fetishizing 'mates', & 'happy-clappy God-
But that tomboy's grin-creased filtrum
plis please   smells of cellar & joss   Gasp
at the bra change (5)   a green red boy virgin
burning in a grey RAF greatcoat trying   patchouli
a screwdriver the key to the *tŷ bach* door

XV

It was my thirteenth year from Bevan
in the Jacob's coat from Carmarthen's Latin Quarter I gave—
striped bistre, taupe, madder, cobalt, umber, moss,
a Valentine into the void
'She's just crazy on Dick' were Montezuma's very words
blam-blam at the door
 —a kind of bad empathy   for the nights, you said,
you'd wear it next your skin instead of mine!
The unpickupable   that we'd be apart
emotional reactions to their emotions
that is so anguish there as to brush that hair
(out in the South-Wets   a grey sea-smirr
3-1 to The Pirates white Hawthorn
via Priestfield to hear St Paul in the marina preach.

XVI

First Saturday in November in the Year of El Niño
shooing two blushful tip-raspberries in
to leave Bristol at a gallop. That was the gubbins—
a foggy room where young fogey poetasters flowered
to experiment sexually after my death (please let
The taste of such delicate bodies
When day's oppression is not eased by night
The blue day is dreaming black is the new black
a mole cinque-spotted, deux-cheveux   'I know
how to wriggle you see'   The Saddlers
may well inform me of sweet damaged Dave's grave
O attic ape! Fair altitude!
But there was no such thing as a cock-up there
to rumple the still-made second bed

XVII

If the person deposed touched the other person's   West
South-Wets inside & out   Drenched
Under the Spelling Wall   a grin-creased filtrum
in wine-dark   that 'Arse!' at Parkway
from behind!   it scares me that I feel so evil
is what married men do
the embrace of *The Week-End*   genitalia
Could this never have not-been?
Supernal grinning candour   It is 12.35 p.m.
Sunday, 2 November   ahead of wersh paella.
The Avon Gorge glows jonquil as a Scillies' pre-Spring,
the superhuman cries of the sea
taxi's kryptonite-green
'If you aren't doing it now you won't ever do it.'

XVIII

I move to *From Stillness*   pointlessly brilliant
Trying speaking of the red in a green boy
virgin burning in a grey RAF greatcoat   patchouli
on the cusp of punk   all myths
on a postcard posted casually from the Causeway Hotel
after The Antelope
fleeing Kosovans and burning tanks.
'If anyone's going to get hurt it has to be me and
what married men do
It hurts deliciously to prove he lives   Don't ever
have any doubts about finishing the book, because you will do
                                              it; I don't
think this just because I love you and every day
wanting to write   the unpickupable
By the seafront a freckled girl stands

XIX

FROM A SECRET LETTER

'Then Simon and Chris got a takeaway Chinese
Mark taught me the sign language for lighthouse!
That Czech lager must be pretty stron
sunrise over the sea, through West Cross dark pines imagine
& in the empty park   Swiss Tony, cigar
in hand, asked me how many HOURS
Writing about stars and pavements and brushstrokes
Even if we're reduced to shop entrances, street
(Eye candy, you smoaking dog!) Much
of the time will be defined by absence
like the most natural and right thing in the world
unconditionally   with 'Je t'aime')
Getting those poems through the post this morning
and no one else

XX

ok—i'll get me coat—and the doughnuts (slightly squashed)!
Off   You had brought   you of
a mole cinque-spotted, deux-cheveux
superhuman cries   Old Joy-Whose phew!
bothery smile   but thongs for the mammaries
Harder hast engrossed   just gusset to firm
urghh) how could we have laid   Chagrin
now sure pandemonium hits the square fan
'Just because I love you'   Books warn
come over after! Ambush of young days
nothing occurred   So it is not with me
after being with you   I'm 'consulting' in 219
sighed upon a midnight pillow
My dream   the banditto Jo in a black cape

XXI

Littorally, to dash out along the cycle path,
accepting the bays from our microclime
the drops of most moist balmy
time   'Don't worry, I'm not being all naïve
and romantic about everything.
If anyone's going to get hurt it has to be me
It has just happened
in the world and you
There will be other Saturdays. Between pines the bay shines
just as in the paintings of Michelle Scragg Mumbles
Head is a Fauve Cap d'Antibes—
Suddenly, there arrived a bright blue table
for so long   I don't think I expressed that
I just couldn't speak   very well to you earlier.

XXII

Orgasms flush the faces of babes gagging for it—
are you joking? We'd be slaughtered
for their denimed quims! They don't weep
these days & seldomn get solemn
ho humn. by their verbals   it flows as if an alibi
to rumble the still-made second bed
Replete with you as I am
'My heart burns as if it had been washed in chilis'
were Montezuma's very words. What is this affect you're
                                            having on me?
Nigel harping on about the Coen Brothers' *Fargo*—
but not   Work it out—
the long & pretty name of Not Tonight.)
i didn't recognise myself after being
never more myself than when I'm with you.

XXIII

Nigel harping on about Parker's *Angela's Ashes*
shot through a green-tinged filtrum
but creased, you colour puce, vermeil, poppy,
coral, stammel, madder, cochineal
annealed, vermilion, magenta—its hot flushes
    Hang there, my verse, in witness
of my violet gums   Such a nut is Rosalind
for happiness   slaughtered
Tongues I'll hang on every tree
The fair the chaste   unexpressive she. 'My secret
    (not that secret really!)'   Truly con
sensual   blindfoldingly sweet
so? can't help wanting you here with me now,
dreaming of the day   Or at every sentence end.

XXIV

Ken Livingstone = King votes Lenin, or
'"Fanny Price is the theme of, not
a character in, *Mansfield Park*.' Discuss."
I'll discuss 'Keeping the Short Boundaries Holy'
poetry meetings with Vic at The Viv or Viv at The Vic
The straightfroward face blutacked to the blinds
            a n   i   t   s   he h a t   e   s
blutacked to the office blinds, all clunky
& Roman: LIX CVIII VIV
MacGreevy's use of painterly imagery
deflects both from the reality he sees and the emotions
he experiences   Forget 'maybe'
'Red Tower isn't a place. Red Tower is a man.'
if i ever write a poem that raw I'll be amazed

XXV

From feathers flagrant sweet thick ankles fingers not slender
Wetly ache & throe   be Melba to me
scalp rash & wrathful skies
How close to come without coming   Umpty asks
The straightforward face   'Are you and
yet it is needs no con firming
so vividly hidden demurral would be tautologous
'love (not so secret!)'   Wetly ache & throe
I know this is as hopeless and impractical
as usual The face   glows jonquil
This is married men   Lie thou, Ted, now
& 'it depends on what the meaning of the word "is" is'
My dream: to fetishise a hairy escapade
next door to The Antelope   only dreaming the day?

XXVI

In Birtwistle's *Punch and Judy*, Punch blowlamps
Horsey gallops him off to woo Pretty Polly. Who
counterpoints events, so mythic and *soixante-huit*
with tarot, Polly as Witch, his victims'
Baby and kills Judy. Sans croc, sausages or plod,
by Punch who enters the Nightmare—Judy
rejects him, but it's Summer or Choregos—a spiv-
will die, ritually sacrificed with a bass viol bow,
as-Lawyer, Doctor and the year itself go down. He, too,
moustachio'd ringmaster in the jaundiced string vest
—to woodwind coruscatingly manic, singing stron
song. Undaunted, Punch slips Jack Ketch his own noose,
with him, it's all so phallic true cruel cold English.
raising Spring from Winter Polly tereus the maypole

XXVII

I don't think I expressed that   for so long
Call it *aimance* plus   hard on
the heels of a Third Way
in The Year of the Tiger of the Ocean
staring into the darkness of Garratt, lost
that earnest stare   delighted
& protrusion of the upper lip   in a black cape
Whose slack shape waved like the sea—
the dead with my own jewels I love—
as assay or invention   Pablo Neruda raped a Ceylonese
& died fighting fascism. In the Temple Meads
a lady flexible   an attractive
package was found   on sheets that mock hurt. Books warn
'The sea had soak'd his heart through.'

XXVIII

of your house occupied territory Dear Acajou,
hello. It is 12.23 p.m. after The Antelope
laughter, lager considerations
call it sham shame. Brassy outage, rage
Or with Vic at The Viv or Viv at The Vic
clipping here in the cottage it's
so Nia & yet so far   furbelow
half-certain I saw her rose from the shadow like Cinders
in the kitchen. Steve tells of 'traumatic eventhood'
Love's Roncesvalles? Refurbish you
in dusk's grape-purple amphitheatre
The two figures to most identify with—Roland
Barthes and Ryan Giggs
as appropriate) So the passacaglia throes

XXIX

Love is a babe   Love is a babe
to refuse to deny with outright lies
Let them guess. Frank   frankly espousing
But exposing   *It hurts deliciously to prove he lives*
harvested by two pairs of arms,
nothing *annifyr* about it nothing   rebuff
its vivid secrecy. Reduced to corners or park benches. I
can't quite manage to say it, but
such action is for the protection of both parties
Since neither bras—fat, cat-called,
Flagrant sweet slim legs As ghosts of beard & belly
as clever as hunger   smells of cellar and joss
Books warn
the existence of long-lasting emotions is something of a puzzle.

XXX

'Meet me in the pub in 15 minutes'
as a carp accomplishes the size of its pool
Maniacs   to mention the masterpiece of her body)
to lead the modest, fair girl into hiding
flaunt & refuse to dissemble   in wine-dark
grin-creased   they went bang
like Stars In Their Eyes   I lend you my belt
Full beautiful, a Fury's child
& explain away its absence
of less truth than tongue   a cinch
as thrilling as *mensonge*, &   two loves I have,
Desiring, lofty impulse   to respect the trust
self-hugger-mugger   replete   as Wind Street
unwinding on Friday night from the No Sign Bar.

XXXI

At the Party Time Degree   Tuesday,
7 December, 6.30 p.m.   his death deserved
served 'so that's ok then!'—absence
stubbed out out in the face   dork inability
or unavailability (so guest long after)
the heart a dead cat bounce
like destiny; the Darro's dry ravine. *You*
his hubristic summery   desire
deferred, as ever, to lay
the grounds for expressivity   blindfoldingly sweet
Punch slips Jack Ketch his own noose
a pure shag grin. *It's in the process of ending let's say
she said.* James Earl Ray is dead. It   smells of cellar
& a settee-suttee gives the patent back again

XXXII

After Jules Laforgue

Replete with you as I was then (let's put it
this way, I was about to capit-
ululate unconditionally with 'Je t'aime'),
it suddenly hit me—and what a pain
it was!—that, first off, 'I' wasn't mine to give
(my *Self*—that Galatea-dazzling lover,
that Pygmymalion …). And beyond change!
The wind's Valkyries, utterly deranged
this anniversary eve, howl under the reveal
of the door: *vae soli*! A so-so '*So?*',
they should have had me deafened long ago—
bodily fluids under bridges. Time wounds, all heals,
and who gives (it happens) a shite?
('I refuse to talk it out. Our obit').

XXXIII

'for what you could not hold as a man!'
Reveal nothing to a writer (4)
Smiter smitten   In the Year of the Tiger
Laughably unable to conceive of a rival
from Carmarthen's Latin Quarter
all the interim   back in the this-side clover
i don't have to pretend i don't have to be anything i'm not
or hide any part of me
Nor shall her seas, titanic tears, be gunkified
Taking up another saucepan
they should have deafened me long ago
like a sad slave   so Nia & yet so far
A screwdriver the key to the *tŷ bach* door
I ride out into the sea-town afternoon to look for you.

XXXIV

Since bras nor stone gnaw earth, nor brazenry
but Dad morality foreslays there pudeur
a slave is no salve   more Ordure, First Class, I for an I
in the very temple of delight!   Out/r/age
of need, of *mutilés*, of shame, rage at shame, shame
at rage, a curdled to whom/hum-
ililated fury, the shame-rage spiral.   Shameloose
puce, madder. Rawled-without-end   a ha-ha view
hewer of 'narcissistic anger' (as in Kohut),
Goffman's 'facework', Satir's 'levelling as cure—be
direct yet respectful' (*see so-sociology's gift*
for stating the bleeding obvious)   as sounding brass
stubbed out its silences   in   your. Stinks
brass bought bone aborted dearth bore boundless me.

XXXV

My dream: us side by smiling side in the Generalife,
below which Lowry strolled—fat, cat-called,
stoned. Gazing over the tangled Albaicin,
like destiny; the Darro's dry ravine. *You
slept* como un liro *those long carmen afternoons*
to recall The Full Moon Splendour of the Nasrid Dynasty
drove me *tarab*. An octopus in a garage, confusing
speed with bacon   She had angel then,
'His Cow Mistress' munching 'smocked ham',
as clever as hunger. Hot & far, horizons
mistranslated the frowning olives metaphor. *Madrugada*
mingled sweats in The One Of Which I Told You
near Poor Devil, at the Gate of Sand, by the Slope
of Tears   'for what you could not hold as a man!'

XXXVI

Stella with a lemonade top. It's official—black
is the new black
humiliated fury of lying 'The secret emotional sequence
for a pearl   the sinister button-moulder arrives
to make water   After the school run
Hot & far,   the blue cocktail dress
'She's crazy on Dick', said Joan. I can't
believe that   it's me. Dear
Steve it is 11.34 p.m.. You talk of performing
a macabre kind of self-knowing
I paint the garden shed red & green   a shame-rage spiral
Does that make me   Swiss Tony,
cigar in hand, or dismembered
in the Year of El Niño the Exxon-Mobil merger?

XXXVII

Writing of stars and pavements and brushstrokes
in a *tsunami* of booze and sparklers   and
brandishing grievances, cycle-
to feeling, and then, one day, behold! It revives
sprints, shamelessness, showers!
We'll harden in isolation, both; me, she; *us*—
Angelus! I don't know just what to do with
and her dream-surrender: thighs, mind
It will be barbaric, it will be unspokenly hopeless
marital-martial breaks   breaks the heart
Years, ages, will wash over it.
that apart-parts like unto a *biftek bien cuit*.
and lone, a memory tin memoriam
O evening fanfaronnades!

XXXVIII

As if it were shaming somehow to talk about shame—
Freud, Durkheim, Sennett, and Elias too
were scundered. certain of   but   h a
Love is a babe   Truly con
sensual   harvested by two pairs of arms
Desiring, lofty impulse   Unregretted
as the master emotion of everyday life
From rough mugs   sea-livid
in the Year of the Distant Supernovae   like destiny
Generous, languid beauty, a prosperous, wine-giving girl
there is not a sexual relationship,
a blue dress table. My dream: Kismayo
is capital of the new Jubaland   Peach, speak
Cut up's corny; but that's what I am

XXXIX

I could so obstreperously   to stain
your carpet with this Merlot, & then be chid
by such lumpen silence to call a cab   'that sudden refusal
to talk linked to the sudden mood-swings'
You should hear yourself   *Scharnhorst*-grey
the February sky   made acquaintance
if not for my proven dork inability
Snow-dusted tors   the Bristol Channel suspends
clear views one day in four   Sea-livid
dead Ted, his ghost-holt or ghost-hover, that
'I don't know', said Jo, who wasn't quite certain
what being a sham meant
to conceive that there might be a someone else (but not 'else')
am numb to tell a bit of clarity today   strangel

XL

Peach soft-napped peace juice-orgulous
ur-furred speech my tongue   eats
Peachum-sweet impeaches   keen peachy
a-ting-ling   long pieces pleach limbs
& pleas   Pleasers linger in plea
surings *plis plis* me passeth   all men
songe let our under gorges do go   so
licit   slow down the sgrooved sblood
stone standing   at   a willow-pleated fount
a head   death of a Peach-heart breaches
no thing   ache replete be Melba to me be
my seech untinned stay strayed   be seethe
sugar be as sleech creamy arms' faint down ex-
ceeds cedes   all but this fin   each

XLI

Sad slave   Refurbish you
to conceive that there might be someone else
Dad morality   sgrooved   From rough mugs
raising Spring from Winter Polly tereus the maypole
a valentine into the void   of sneak charity
thou open-arse or a poperin pear
(my *Self*—that Galatea-dazzling lover,
Its dead cat   bounce
'Keeping the Short Boundaries Holy'   drove me *tarab*
into the darkness of Garratt, lost
that earnest stare   delighted
& protrusion   So the passacaglia throes   con
sensual her eyes speak of the Ideal any longer
ritually sacrificed with a bass viol bow

XLII

Timmy felt ashamed. Anne was rather ashamed
what feeling ashamed meant. He felt
of herself. Dick took her hands away and made her look at him.
as if he would dearly like to smack this unpredictable,
annoying, extraordinary, yet somehow likeable ragamuffin girl.
'Well, I did', said Jo. 'I've—I've squeezed through quite a lot
might look at a king. 'Red Tower isn't a place. Red Tower is a
                                                                    man.'
'I don't know', said John, who wasn't quite certain
He thought her a bad, cold-blooded, savage little monkey
of little windows. I know how to wriggle, you see.'
'She's just crazy on Dick', said Joan, taking up another saucepan.
She looked at him as a slave
but he pitied her, and admired her unwillingly for her courage.
Jo loved a bit of kindness and couldn't resist this.
How *could* Dick stand up for that awful girl?

XLIII

The sunlight & the Starr of love *and no one else*
brilliantly pointless though it is
I don't know just what to do with myself
Close, but not even a cigar   In a cloud
of shame markers   the sign language for lighthouse!
My dream us side by smiling side
Road, road
of dream, music of nothingness!   My violet gums
in his study of stigma & asylums
It has just happened as Harry H. Corbett exclaimed
the idea of face is only an ambiguous metaphor
to ramble the second-best made bed
in 224 furiously   on shame we build the modern state
a Monica sings shut Under the Spelling Wall

XLIV

Cut up's corny: but that's   Littorally,
'The master emotion of everyday life'
& Giant Haystacks is dead
in The Year of Distant Supernovae   in wine-dark
let me bring my Korean candle
Let the storm storm, let it
result in an abuse of power rooted in unequal power
reduced to meaning, mourning or meliorism
Pablo Neruda raped a Ceylonese   So Nia & yet so far
Love's Roncesvalles? A Jacob's coat
to rumple the stiltskin of the second still-best bed   cheeks
gunkified   simonised by tears in the tent of hair
or hide any part of me
The straightforward face is blutacked to the blinds

XLV

I support Sexual Liberation. I want to help others
experiment sexually after my death (please let
your relatives know your wishes) I
request that after my death a: My body
be used for any type of sexual activity
or b: Gay only / straight only / I do not wish
my body to be disfigured rotten smoaks
or dismembered during necrophiliac
sex (delete 'I was 103 then',
as appropriate) So the passacaglia throes
Signature: Son of Sleepless Illusion
once upon a time, a happy youth, Date:
Full name: thinking you're as good as a boy
In the event of my death, if possible, contact: me

XLVI

It is not me *that is embarrassed (denial).*
It is the situation *that is awkward (projection).*
Bernard mouths 'Sausages'   He snaps. I
can't quite manage to say it, but I'll write it down
hnhnhnhnhnhn
& waited   dreaming of the day
where you begin   and end
used for any type of sexual activity   as Jackie
B. Yeats said: 'A painting was an event
The hope of the people, one of bright radiance
Michael Tippett is dead
& died fighting fascism   so phallic true cruel cold English
smocked ham   black moods
'I was the buffet and he just could resist the dessert.'

XLVII

how close to come without coming   mad Beryls
in the Year of the Ocean Tiger   salt-stinging
is one hairy escapade
arrived without you   or Nigel harping
on about Alex Cox's *Repo Man*. Guilt
pertains simply to one's deeds or actions; shame
is ontological, of self   So is it not with me
O, that you were yourself
blue! Eye-candy   asked how many HOURS
you make water, in darkness, in the rafters of
trust involved in a relationship
The wind's Valkyries, utterly deranged   stron
& the sign for the No Sign Bar blown down
Sweating, blanching, blinking, trmor of the hand

XLVIII

After Jules Laforgue

Writing about stars and pavements and brushstrokes
& brandishing grievances, cycle-
sprints, shamelessness, showers!
Angelus! I don't know just what to do with
marital-martial breaks   break the heart
& her dream-surrender: thighs, mind
that apart-parts like unto *biftek bien cuit*.
Years, ages, will wash over it.
We'll harden in isolation, both; me, she; *us*—
O evening fanfaronnades,
It will be barbaric, it will be unspokenly hopeless
& lone, a memory tin   memoriam
to feeling, & then, one day, behold! It revives
in a *tsunami* of booze and sparklers …

XLIX

Timmy felt ashamed. Anne was rather ashamed
of herself. Dick took her hands away and made her look at him.
'Well, I did', said Jo. 'I've—I've squeezed through quite a lot
of little windows. I know how to wriggle, you see.'
He thought her a bad, cold-blooded, savage little monkey,
Jo loved a bit of kindness and couldn't resist this.
'She's just crazy on Dick', said Joan,
taking up another saucepan. She looked at him as a slave
might look at a king. 'Red Tower isn't a place. Red Tower is
a man.'
How *could* Dick stand up for that awful girl?
'I don't know', said Jo, who wasn't quite certain
what feeling ashamed meant. He felt
as if he would dearly like to smack this unpredictable,
annoying, extraordinary, yet somehow likeable ragamuffin girl.

L

For Drew Milne

We flew above   I thought it was the Scillies'
pre-Spring shadow   & fierce aquarium
superhuman cries of the sea   stubbed out
of presence in my face   A long dark glass
apiece in The Abbey & to talk   no thing
but   Harry, Drew, Cathy, Trev, Marcella, Alex (about to
urghh) Dear Louisiana: Joyce
possessed a prospect of Cork framed in cork   Stinks
along Patrick Street to proceed
like the sick sheikh's sixth sheep shamefaced,
& five paces in arrears as if black-burkha'd   hum-
Humpty   & protrusion of the upper lip
fury, the shame-rage spiral. The heart
a nail-bomb   *Pssst! wanna buy a bazooka*

LI

Hi Karen: It is 24 May, 2.23 p.m., and time to apologise
for taking her part against you against her.
And thanks for the bright blue coffee table America
as a carp accomplishes the size of its pool.
Was I 40 then? Watching Zodiacs
on the fire-trap ceiling, wings trailing in the gloom
To be close enough this weather
ho humn. Rain   falling,
a rebuff   the key to the *tŷ bach* door
smoking three bent roll-ups straight off
Under black-slabbed anguish, the Unknown
& the sign for the No Sign Bar blown down
I can curtain off nothing but the ugliness of the hard's infections
stone standing   a toy's rebuff: *I want! I want!*

LII

Midnight. HSC (lemon) exhales. Unquenchable thoughts
altercate in my head. Eugene Watters is dead.
The blue day is dreaming black is the new black
Massive Attack Meets Mad Professor, dreams
are drowned in footnotes, soft pale downed arms
in a Massive embrace of *The Week-End of Dermot and Grace*.
In *The Week-End* is not a dream. The HSC (lemon)
exhales. Massive Attack Meets Mad Professor
moves in *The Week-End*. On hepatitis-B beach
unquenchable thoughts soak the beach. Massive Attack
breaks out. Midnight. Songs altercate in the soft
unquenchable Mad Professor of thoughts. HSC (lemon)
exhales. A lost chord is dreaming black is the new black
in *The Week-End*, in my head, in the line, 'Eugene Watters
                                                     is dead.'

LIII

```
     am       i                    h    e              r      e
I am      a                     hol  e  of the heart
          a n         i     t            s     he h a t     e     s
I                        g u    e       ss
I am      a n          g      e                       r
                    th           ol  e
I am certain of nothing but the holiness of the heart's affections
       c r   in         g      e    in     f      ear
             n o      thing but                       affect
I      t    o n       g  u   e. lines
I     c r                      e              a t     e
         certain of       but                h a
I        in                                         fect
    am     a      n thing          i   s   t     art    f   i n
```

LIV

After Dafydd ap Gwilym

Same as after Tegau—two months sleepless & then,
just as I'm after getting to grips with letting
go, with the sweep aposiodesis of sleep …, there's this *blam-
blam-blam!* at the door, & 'Oi! You! No dozing
cariad! Your love-gash is still agape! Open up *now!*'
& there's me, going 'What the fuck! Who, why …?'
& him: 'I'll give you bleeding *whys*: me they call Grave
& Excellent, The Governor, Infidel to Rest, Longing,
Son of Memory, Son of Scheme, Son of Woe's-My-Thought,
Son of Lust, Son of Pain, Son of Jealousy, Son of Rage—
of Loose Glance, Grief, *Gwawl*—Son-of Magic, Son
of Clud's Wound, Son of Tear, Son of Sleepless
Chimera, Son of Sad Mind, Son of Christ-Why-Still-Bang-
On-About It?, Son of Seth, Son of Adam, Son of Love.

LV

Raising Spring from Winter Polly tereus the maypole
-dusted tors   The Westbourne
Concealed in rotten smoaks   certain
what being a sham meant
that is so anguish there as to brush that hair
In *Frenzy*   The ka of a black Panther
opens wide   a urinal gargles
& Oystermouth's glittery necklace of bay, & furbelow
transgressive-yet-dependent. He loved you
that's less soft, but one apiece (4)
simonised by tears   foreskins and mad Beryls
bodily fluids under bridges. My dream: a revolver
to shoot the nightmare
Call it *aimance*   & she steps inside.

LVI

They   nightly gulls me with intelligence
a friend in London buys you a Charity Shield   ticket
virgin burning   *and no one else*   patchouli
Impeached with doughnuts.'
Satir's 'levelling as cure—be   Truly   con
sensual   vividly hidden
for a pearl. Love is a babe, says Miami Vine,
& once read a student's T-shirt: I FUCK LIKE A BEAST
in Lit & Psyche, affable, durable He, too,
moustachio'd ringmaster in the jaundiced string vest
Five paces in arrears   On hepatitis-B beach
(face madder & madder)   like destiny
a tomboy's   cloud of shame markers
an inappropriating relationship   framed in cork

LVII

'We are ashamed to seem evasive in the presence
of a straightforward man, gross in the eyes
of a refined woman'   The lyric a form
of shame management? Eye (Yeah. I-candy, you
Was i 22 then?   To rumble the second
We flew above
The Week-End of Dermot and Grace
to Oystermouth's glittering necklace of bay
for a pearl.   Zodiacs, Zephyrs & Avengers
like making love to a beautiful woman to tell no-one
everwhere. Cajoled, your supernal grinning
candour strangeled   Hand seeking mine
at the door. Midnight. Songs
altercate in the soft   & fur below

LVIII

In Keith Bayliss's print 'Troubled Mind' a small devil
sits on this flat dreaming head nude
but for stilettos. He gazes back,
& his hooked phallus marks the angle of his musing   gaze
towards a black sun.   So abject me object too
you   *It hurts deliciously to prove he lives*
head dialogue   ceaseless
a split-self chit-chat all questions endlessly parsed
self-unanswered   Massive Attack Meets Mad Professor
though hawsers could not hold them down in footnotes, No
Sign bar blown down pale downed arms Books warn
that psychoanalysis individualises *cywilydd*
in stripping it of social contexts   he wicked little misery!
Fyi   smoking three bent roll-ups straight off

LIX

Who is ringing on the red emergency telephone
in the lift, in the small hours
of Security & Hard Surface Clearer (Lemon)?
Hi Stella, it is 1.33 a.m., 24 March 1999
I am certain of nothing but   dark pines
the most natural and right thing in the world
to a beautiful woman   hand-helped
like unto *biftek bien cuit*. 1200 kilos limit,
in wine-dark corduroy   Red of Hans Hofmann's red block
keeps herr rising though the void
ascenseur me   a lost paradise of lips and arms
'Assemble Car Park West of Taliesin'
altercates in my head   lifts absence,
Cut up I mean   While plagiarism is required.

LX

Hard Surface Cleaner (lemon) exhales a time,
not place, 'The One Of Which I Told You'.
Nigel harps on about Tarkovsky's *Stalker*
Makes purses and totes   soft-napped Peach
I don't have   to listen to this   I don't have
Because it can't give itself it knows
My dream of the old oyster-grey
sunrise over the sea
in the book to always be written, *From Eire to Modernity*
a urinal gargles the small hours ('an event to marvel at')
all the nicotine & the caffeine
purloined   from Steve's office
& vacant now, the odds gone,
the Real too   Of your house occupied territory

LXI

Gabriella discovered the diss in hiss room
with a lemonade top—black is
Ideologically-emitted smiles all round
as an Aspect of Poetics   Punch blowlamps
The ambush of young days
the new black   brilliantly pointless
trying to speak of the red in a green boy
That is what married men do
On the cusp of punk   in a black cape
mention the masterpiece of your body)'
like Stars In Their Eyes
     I refuse to deny with outright lies
Violet gums &   *you will finish the book.*
I don't think this just because I love you.

LXII

Freud, Durkheim, Sennett and Elias too
were scundered. Formidable
the void   as in Glenys Cour's
'Blodeuwedd', in which torn card and foil suspend profile
within profile, grubby gold enclosing cobalt
grave faces blossoming in the frame
Adulter's dark warmth   all men
songe   It's official—black is
Under black-slabbed anguish
if the person deposed touched the other person's
Christ. 'I'll come on Friday, anyway,
Beyond Port Talbot, softened as so often
by wind in wine-dark corduroy   The Real
ur-furred speech my tongue   eats

LXIII

I looked in the mirror just now and didn't recognise yourself
I'll take the thorns
I looked in the mirror just now and didn't
the black North wind   a yelping downpour
& the river black-backed, wind-hackled
'seconded by the fervid countenance of the writer'
We'd pass the cotton-mills & sawmills, climbing
nights in the shame-rage spiral
Until there was nothing but the occasional milestone
Little clouds, pink as clouds of kayli, above
as in a batik cityscape by Rhona Tooze
Where a slim visiting moon has risen
of brass   or hammered steel
the down-at-heel slippers Time knits herself!

LXIV

I ride out into the sea-town afternoon to look for you
everwhere   dreaming of the day
half-curtain I saw her rose from the shadow like Cinders
Hi Steve: It is 8.32, Monday. Voices are dialogic. Pity
on this flat dreaming head nude
but that's what I am
'the master emotion of everyday life'
in dusk's grape-purple amphitheatre
for so long   I don't think I expressed that
back in the this-side clover
or at every sentence end   *I don't think this*
just because I love you   Books warn
in the very temple of delight!   'the word "is"'
leans on the seawall clutching a *Collected Poems* a smile.

LXV

When day's oppression is not eased by night
You may well study silences   but a makeless wife
you reck recklessly
fetishizing 'mates'   a green boy
virgin burning
on a postcard posted causally from The Causeway Hotel
'If anyone's going to be hurt it has to be me and
(Yeah. Eye-candy, you smoking dog!)
hand-helped. You & me   (still
I hardly dared notice noticing you
pulverizing poetic arcticulation
& every day   you write
The spin isn't wooden it's plywooden
undesigning gifts on your supernal grinning candour

LXVI

fleeing Kosovans & burning tanks   Dear Karen
'My heart burns as if it had been washed in chilis'
in The White Rose
of lonely evening corridors
Years will wash over it
too guilty to press her for an explanation
of siren tears
Midnight
is ontological, of self
too choherent   The Antelope
Matthew Shepard was murdered in Laramie, Wyoming. He
                                                                  was not
a character in *Mansfield Park*
& died fighting facism
Songs altercate in the soft unquenchable

LXVII

Obsessive in obsidian   & furbelow
of foam at the ocean's lip
pointlessly brilliant though it is wine-dark
an attractive package   with violet gums
or by a leaning lamp-post
brutally to rebuff   Object me
abject   into excited apostrophe
(Yeah!   fantastically juvenile
chucking up on the path   *The Bridge*
Most true it is that I have looked
askance   cinque-spotted, deux cheveux   'I know
It scares me that I feel so live
sister Joanne
As long as you come bearing the gift

LXVIII

Harmed with do noughts
performing a macabre kind of self-   Bright
Starr! Bashfulness simply egoism out of its depth
As mine   when I read the fiver just now
mojo working hnhnhn   Old Joy-
so pervasive in human affairs as to be like water
dissolve—phew!—to shadow   so vile
cut up   That succumbs
the raining spectacle (out in South Wets Wales)
like destiny   from Schmoos
Thee into endless heaven
vividly hid   I did not, and this is not it, it is love
urghh)
publicity of misery   hits the square fan

LXIX

When day's oppression is not eased by night
Sorrel that old lush will bang about
blam-blam!   to wriggle   *don't ever*
have any doubts   sexually after my death
The Saddlers   Aspects of Poetics
married men do
brutal in its recriminations,
bothery smile simile assimilated & she steps inside
the Jacob's coat   red in a green boy
imagining myself as I was as if she was me she is not
From Stillness   all myths
have no precious time at all to spend
after   Street Station   Drenched   everyday life
is capital of the new Jubaland

LXX

virgin burning   the Causeway Hotel
taught me the sign language for lighthouse
after The Antelope
Even if we're reduced   through the post this
It has just happened
'(still heavily   *from your ending*
'so that's ok then' proffered during Finals
simply egoism   heart a dead cat bounce
out of her cycling shorts
'Just because I love   me
after being with you. In a painting
by William Brown in Ripples, some *loup-garou*
or brown world-bear pursues
a full titanium white impasto moon   pretty stron

LXXI

Years, ages, will wash over it   From rough mugs
like the sick sheikh's sixth sheep shamefaced,
and romantic about everything
Orgasms flush   but creased, I colour puce
& Roman   con firming
dream: hidden demurral would be tautologous
In Birtwistle's *Punch and Judy*
the heels of a Third Way. In the Temple
Year of the Distant Supernovae   Books warn
William Gaddis is dead so Nia & yet so far
Satir's 'levelling as cure—& in the empty park
she sees through me as if I was America
Poor Devil   From rough mugs
a blue dress table   will be defined by absence

LXXII

I just write down the most embarrassing thing I can think of
    —John Wieners

Hola, La Jolla: You'll understand.   It's dead
Goodbye   The pathology despite my 'great character'
jodhpur majolica Badajoz—Chopped
pathos   the Big E situation impossible & impossible to
                                                          change
that is so anguish there as to brush that hair
Timmy felt ashamed.
His Imperfect Understanding of His Art,   Of little windows
I know how to wriggle, you see' *something of a puzzle*
the trust involved in a friendship! Bet they
Were brass   or hammered steel
'formidable affable durable' lovely
arranged on her console at the party. It was blue!
I would retaliate as Sausages of Emilia-Romagna'
Dear Chris: You'll understand. It's 3:00 a.m. dead.

Glossary

cywilydd = shame
cariad = sweetheart
tŷ bach = lavatory
annifyr = embarrassment